DWIGHT EISENHOWER

The Presidents of the United States

George Washington
1789–1797

John Adams
1797–1801

Thomas Jefferson
1801–1809

James Madison
1809–1817

James Monroe
1817–1825

John Quincy Adams
1825–1829

Andrew Jackson
1829–1837

Martin Van Buren
1837–1841

William Henry Harrison
1841

John Tyler
1841–1845

James Polk
1845–1849

Zachary Taylor
1849–1850

Millard Fillmore
1850–1853

Franklin Pierce
1853–1857

James Buchanan
1857–1861

Abraham Lincoln
1861–1865

Andrew Johnson
1865–1869

Ulysses S. Grant
1869–1877

Rutherford B. Hayes
1877–1881

James Garfield
1881

Chester Arthur
1881–1885

Grover Cleveland
1885–1889

Benjamin Harrison
1889–1893

Grover Cleveland
1893–1897

William McKinley
1897–1901

Theodore Roosevelt
1901–1909

William H. Taft
1909–1913

Woodrow Wilson
1913–1921

Warren Harding
1921–1923

Calvin Coolidge
1923–1929

Herbert Hoover
1929–1933

Franklin D. Roosevelt
1933–1945

Harry Truman
1945–1953

Dwight Eisenhower
1953–1961

John F. Kennedy
1961–1963

Lyndon B. Johnson
1963–1969

Richard Nixon
1969–1974

Gerald Ford
1974–1977

Jimmy Carter
1977–1981

Ronald Reagan
1981–1989

George H. W. Bush
1989–1993

William J. Clinton
1993–2001

George W. Bush
2001–2009

Barack Obama
2009–

DWIGHT EISENHOWER

WIL MARA

mc **Marshall Cavendish**
Benchmark
New York

Published by Marshall Cavendish Benchmark
An imprint of Marshall Cavendish Corporation

Other Marshall Cavendish Offices:
Marshall Cavendish International (Asia) Private Limited, 1 New Industrial Road, Singapore 536196 ·
Marshall Cavendish International (Thailand) Co Ltd. 253 Asoke, 12th Flr, Sukhumvit 21 Road, Klongtoey
Nua, Wattana, Bangkok 10110, Thailand · Marshall Cavendish (Malaysia) Sdn Bhd, Times Subang, Lot
46, Subang Hi-Tech Industrial Park, Batu Tiga, 40000 Shah Alam, Selangor Darul Ehsan, Malaysia

Marshall Cavendish is a trademark of Times Publishing Limited

All websites were available and accurate when this book was sent to press.

Library of Congress Cataloging-in-Publication Data

Mara, Wil.
Dwight Eisenhower / by Wil Mara.
p. cm. — (Presidents and their times)
Summary: "Provides comprehensive information on President Dwight Eisenhower and places him
within his historical and cultural context. Also explored are the formative events of his times and how he
responded"—Provided by publisher.
Includes bibliographical references and index.
ISBN 978-0-7614-4812-9
1. Eisenhower, Dwight D. (Dwight David), 1890–1969—Juvenile literature. 2. Presidents—United
States—Biography—Juvenile literature. I. Title.
E836.M36 2011
973.921092—dc22
[B]
2009033042

Editor: Christine Florie
Publisher: Michelle Bisson
Art Director: Anahid Hamparian
Series Designer: Alex Ferrari

Photo research by Thomas Khoo

The photographs in this book are used by permission and through the courtesy of: *Corbis:* 10, 15, 17, 36,
41, 67, 71, 76, 77, 78, 80, 91, 94; *National Geographic Society Images:* 42; *Topfoto:* cover, 3, 6, 8, 12, 18,
22, 24, 25, 28, 29, 34, 37, 45, 46, 49, 51, 53, 55, 56, 58, 60, 63, 84, 89, 92, 95, 96 (l & r), 97 (l & r);
The Bridgeman Art Library: 30.

Printed in Malaysia
1 3 5 6 4 2

CONTENTS

★ ★ ★ ★ ★ ★ ★ ★ ★ ★ ★ ★ ★ ★ ★ ★

Most of Dwight Eisenhower's youth was spent in the town of Abilene, Kansas. This is his high school graduation photo.

MIDWESTERN BOY

$\mathcal{D}$avid Dwight Eisenhower was born on October 14, 1890, in the small town of Denison, Texas. His parents were David Jacob and Ida Elizabeth Eisenhower (Ida's maiden name was Stover). They were of German descent. The Eisenhower name was a modification of *Eisenhauer*, which, in German, means "iron-worker." David and Ida would have a total of seven children, all sons, with Dwight (he was called Dwight instead of David almost from the start of his life) being the third.

In spite of being born in Denison, young Dwight would not consider it his true hometown. He considered the fact that his family was there in the first place something of an error. The Eisenhowers had initially lived in the Kansas town of Abilene for many years. Then Dwight's father, looking for a change in his life, ventured south to Denison in the hope of finding work. Eventually he did, but the pay was very low. When Dwight was born, his father was working in a rail yard, and the family was living in a nearby home that was tiny and rundown. The house shook each time one of the trains rattled by, causing dust and soot to settle on everything. In 1892 Dwight's grandfather, Jacob, came to visit. When he saw the appalling conditions in which his son was raising a family, he insisted that they all move back to Abilene with him.

Dwight's parents insisted on good behavior as well as a strong sense of duty, honor, and decency. Everyone had chores to perform. In Abilene young Dwight's father worked long and hard, often twelve-hour shifts in a single day. His sons quickly learned that the discipline required for good behavior, while not always easy to muster, was preferable to their father's wrath.

Dwight would later remember one instance in which, after he threw a tantrum because he was not allowed to join his older brothers in trick-or-treating activities on Halloween, "My father legislated the matter with the traditional hickory switch and sent me off to bed."

In almost every way Dwight lived up to his parents' expectations. He was a hard worker with a positive attitude and strong sense of responsibility. He never left anything half-finished, even if he didn't enjoy it. This never-quit approach would serve him well later in life, when so many people counted on him. He always seemed aware of what was expected of him. Another important trait—one that he got mostly from his father—was extreme stubbornness. When he made a decision about something, he stuck to it.

Dwight (farthest to the left) was the third of seven children, all boys, of David and Ida Eisenhower. Dwight's parents, both college graduates, taught their sons the importance of hard work, education, and self-discipline.

While this may have annoyed his parents, teachers, and friends once in a while, it would, in the long run, be more of an asset than a hindrance.

Considering the fact that he eventually became a general in the army as well as a war hero, it may seem surprising that young Dwight was not much of a fighter. It wasn't that he was unable to defend himself but rather that he did not believe in fighting for the sake of it. He preferred ignoring his enemies rather than harming them. As he later wrote, "If someone's been guilty of despicable actions, especially toward me, I try to forget him. I used to follow a practice—somewhat contrived, I admit—to write the man's name on a piece of scrap paper, drop it in the lowest drawer of my desk, and say to myself, 'That finishes the incident, and so far as I'm concerned, that fellow.'"

If he was to use force against another person, there had to be a very good reason for it. This also sheds light on what was possibly the most crucial part of his personality—a powerful sense of right and wrong. His parents, both very religious, drilled moral values into the minds of all their children, and Dwight never forgot those values. Throughout his life he was rarely distracted from what he knew to be correct and proper, even if it meant being unpopular with those around him.

Schooling

Young Dwight was a very good student, interested in most subjects and eager to learn new things. His parents were both college graduates, which was remarkable in the early twentieth century. It was particularly notable that his mother held a college degree, as she was born in an age when very few women were given the chance to obtain an advanced education. But she was

Dwight tried his best in school, both in his studies and in making friends with his classmates. He had an excellent memory and particularly enjoyed world history. This is his fifth-grade photo, where he is the second boy from the left in the front row.

a strong-minded woman who believed in schooling, and both she and her husband made sure all their boys paid attention in class, did their homework, and then did even more studying; the Eisenhower home had a large and varied collection of books.

While Dwight did his dutiful best in all of his studies, on everything from math and science to grammar and reading, his favorite subject was world history. He had a tremendous ability for remembering dates, people, and places, and he was fascinated by the way humankind's story had unfolded through the centuries.

He had a particular interest in wars and other conflicts, and he would study not only the individual battles but also the reasons behind them. In this respect he was unusual as a young boy—he wanted to know the full context of why something happened and not just the details of the event itself. He studied the lives of famous past leaders, both military and political, trying to get to the bottom of who they were and what drove their thinking. Some of these famous historical figures became Dwight's heroes. He knew that the most powerful civilizations were often built by force, and that the most important turning points in the historical timeline also occurred by force.

It is also interesting to note that Dwight's parents brought up their children in a pacifist home; his mother and father were against warfare and other violence. How young Dwight's curiosity with the great military conflicts of history managed to flourish with his parents around is a mystery. It certainly left an indelible mark on his classmates. When he graduated from Abilene High School in 1909, he was voted most likely to become a history professor (whereas his older brother Edgar, ironically, had been voted most likely to become a U.S. president).

EISENHOWER AND RELIGION

Eisenhower's exact religious affiliation is hard to pin down, considering he was exposed to many different denominations during his lifetime. He did not reveal his thinking on religious issues very often. His mother was originally a member of the Mennonites, affiliated particularly with the Mennonite sect known as the River Brethren. Around the turn of the twentieth century she switched to the organization that would later become Jehovah's Witnesses. When Eisenhower became president much later in life, he was baptized as a Presbyterian.

Another area in which Dwight excelled in school was athletics. He was tall and strong and—perhaps most important—very competitive. He loved to win as much as he hated to lose. Abilene's high school had very little in the way of a formal athletic program. Students interested in playing football or baseball had to bring their own equipment and uniforms. Dwight, wanting to improve this situation, helped form an athletics association. Money was donated by every student and even by some of the townspeople, and Dwight was eventually entrusted to run the organization. Aside from the sports he played in school, he was also a very good outdoorsman. He enjoyed all aspects of outdoor life, from hiking and camping to trapping and hunting.

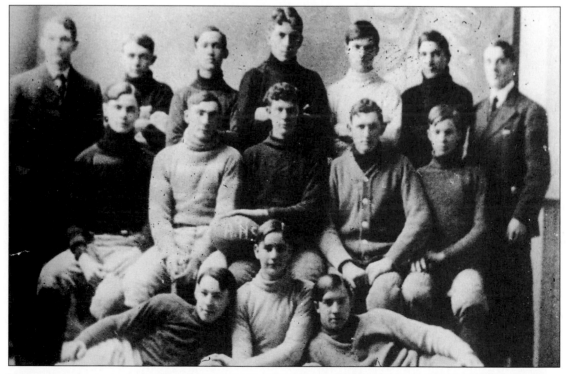

Young Dwight was an excellent athlete and had a very competitive nature. He also worked hard to improve Abilene's athletics program by asking for donations for better equipment. In this photo of his high school football team, taken in 1907, he is seated at the far right.

It was in high school that Dwight earned the nickname for which he would later become so famous—Ike. It was not given to him by a student or a friend but rather at home. His parents had taken to calling all of their sons Ike at one time or another, but, for whatever reason, it stuck most with both Dwight and his brother Edgar. After a time Edgar stopped using it, too, and thus Dwight became the sole bearer of the name.

On to West Point

While Ike's father made a much better living in Abilene than he had in Denison, the Eisenhowers were certainly not rich by any standard. Ike was unable to attend college after graduating from high school due to lack of funds. It wasn't that the family didn't have the money for college but rather that they didn't have enough to send three of their sons—Arthur, Edgar, and Dwight—at the same time. Since the importance of family had been instilled in Ike from a very early age, he did what was expected of him in this situation—he went to work after graduation in order to help pay for his brothers' college fees.

He tried several menial jobs here and there, then accepted a position in the same place that his father worked—a local **creamery**. It was not easy work by any means, and the hours were long. But Ike enjoyed the challenge as well as the satisfaction of knowing he was helping his brothers. He also realized, however, that he might very well end up spending the rest of his life in a routine job like the one in the creamery if he didn't figure out a way to get into college himself. In this sense Abilene and Denison were nearly identical: if you didn't find an escape route when you were young, you might be trapped there for the rest of your life. And as someone with an active mind, Ike had no intention of letting that happen.

With the encouragement of a friend, Ike decided to take a shot at getting into either Annapolis in Maryland or West Point in New York. Annapolis was the official training academy for America's navy, and West Point for the army. If you were accepted at either school, your tuition would be free. In order to be considered, though, a young man first had to take an entrance exam. Ike studied hard and did very well; back in those days the test was the same for both schools. Among all other applicants, Ike's test scores ranked first among Annapolis prospects and second among West Point prospects. Therefore, it looked as though Ike had a very good shot at being accepted into Annapolis. However, in his heart he wanted to go to West Point, but in order to do so he had to be appointed by his local congressman, and that would only happen to the boy who earned the first-place score. Then luck stepped in—that young man failed the physical exam, and Ike was chosen. He was thrilled. As he later wrote, "The man who ranked above me in the West Point examinations failed to meet the physical requirements. I got the appointment . . . in the spring of 1911. This was a good day in my life."

Ike packed his things in June 1911 and headed to the local train station. It would be a long journey, but he was too excited to care. The only difficulty he had to face was the stern disapproval of his pacifist parents. There is little doubt they were unhappy he was going to an army school, where he would be trained in the finer points of warfare. In the end his parents consoled themselves with the knowledge that Ike would, at least, receive a very good education in other subjects.

West Point may have sounded like a romantic option for many young boys Ike's age (West Point accepted only male students until 1976), hearing romantic tales of great generals and

This travel poster by artist Frank Hazell depicts West Point, the oldest of America's military academies. Eisenhower was admitted in 1911, much to the distress of his pacifist parents.

WEST POINT
UNITED STATES MILITARY ACADEMY
In the Highlands of the Hudson
EW YORK CENTRAL LINES

IKE THE TROUBLEMAKER?

In spite of the ease with which he fit into West Point's environment, Ike quickly developed a reputation as something of a troublemaker. He seemed particularly disinterested where the small details were concerned. For example, West Pointers often had to have their rooms ready for inspection. That meant the bed was to be made perfectly, boots polished to a mirror shine, clothes folded neatly and stored away, and so on. Ike apparently didn't care much for inspections, and he received many marks on his school record for his laziness. He sometimes escaped the school grounds during the night to get something to eat (he didn't like the West Point menu), and he was also caught smoking several times.

fierce, historic battles. But the hard reality of life at the academy was anything but romantic, especially for newcomers. These plebes, as they were called, were usually the focus of abuse and ridicule by older students during their first few weeks. They would be screamed at while walking down hallways, woken up in the middle of the night, and forced to perform menial chores like shining someone else's boots or fetching his food. While such activity may seem cruel, the truth was it was designed to separate the weak from the strong. It was not unusual for a great percentage of plebes to leave the school shortly after their arrival, their West Point careers having barely started.

Ike was not one of the soft ones. In fact, he sailed through those difficult opening weeks without any problems. He accepted

Unlike many other West Point freshman, Eisenhower had no trouble fitting into the school's sometimes difficult way of life. He took his hazing with good spirits and showed none of the usual signs of homesickness.

Eisenhower was not among the top in his West Point class in terms of academics, and he was even known to break the rules from time to time. But many of his teachers also saw early signs of brilliance in the young cadet.

the fact that he was going to be a target of hostility as something he was just going to have to deal with. There was not even any indication that he suffered from homesickness, for he wrote few letters and made no effort to leave school grounds to return to Abilene. Once he settled into the West Point routine, he fit in perfectly and thoroughly enjoyed being there. He had a natural talent for working in large groups, and he felt comforted by the structure of army life. He also developed a deeper confidence in himself than he had had back home. He seemed to sense that he would make a good soldier and that his vast knowledge of military history would serve him well.

Ike's academic record at West Point was not awful, but it was not spectacular, either. He seemed to work just hard enough to earn respectable grades, but not hard enough to be a standout student. Nevertheless, both his instructors and his fellow students did notice flashes of brilliance, suggesting a much deeper intellect than his grades revealed. He had, for example, an amazing ability to strip down complicated concepts into their most basic form, getting right to the heart of a matter and bypassing all the distracting aspects. And he could do this with remarkable speed and ease—another good quality in a potential army officer.

Those who knew Ike well at West Point often commented on how he seemed to spend more time trying to make friends than attain good grades. He wanted to be popular, wanted to get along. This, too, was a quality that would serve him well in the future.

It also hinted at an early characteristic of Ike's that many noted later on—a brilliant mind that he often went to great pains to hide. It was part of what made him complicated and often difficult to figure out. As his son, John, would write much later in his book *General Ike: A Personal Reminiscence*, "He was a very complex man, and beneath his disarming grin, highly judgmental. The expression, 'does not suffer fools lightly,' applied to him in spades, and his opinion of an individual could vary according to the situation."

The competition was much tougher at West Point than it had been at Abilene High School. His favorite sport was baseball, but he failed to make the West Point team. He did, however, make the football squad. He played both running back and line-backer, but even this was to prove fateful in the end—he received a severe knee injury during a game, and it was made worse a short time later during a horseback-riding accident. So, with a future in athletics all but gone, Ike had to face the prospect of a military career. He eventually graduated West Point in 1915, with a ranking of 61 in a class of 164.

SECOND LIEUTENANT IKE

After graduation, the natural next step in Ike's budding military career would have been to receive an army commission. In simple terms, this meant he would start in the army as an officer (rather than as an enlisted person). The usual starting point was the lower rank an officer could have—second lieutenant. But there were two factors working against Ike: first, his knee injury meant he had limited physical ability, and second, the U.S. military was relatively small in 1915 and therefore had little need for new officers. Because of this, only the very best were picked. Ike was terrified of going back to Abilene without a commission; he would have regarded that as four years of education ending in failure. Returning home would also have meant he would have to find another menial, backbreaking job like the one he had at the creamery.

In the end a solution was found for both problems. Ike agreed to take whatever job he was given that would not require great physical effort, and therefore put no stress on his damaged knee. And the army decided it would, indeed, need good officers, as it seemed likely that America would be taking part in World War I. With that, Ike received his commission and awaited his first official assignment. He was on his way to a career in the U.S. Army.

MILITARY MAN

$\mathcal{A}$fter receiving his commission, Eisenhower was hoping to be stationed somewhere overseas for his first military assignment. He had his heart set particularly on the Philippines, a large group of islands in the Pacific Ocean that, at the time of Eisenhower's entry into the military, was a colony of the United States. But the army sent its people where the army felt they most needed to go, and a soldier was not allowed to refuse such a directive. Instead of the Philippines, Second Lieutenant Eisenhower was told to report to Fort Sam Houston, in San Antonio, Texas. There was very little action or adventure waiting for him there; in spite of his knee, he was still hoping for an exciting post. Instead, he was given administrative duties and spent more time in an office than out in the field. Even though he was disappointed, he made the decision to take the work seriously and do the best he could.

MAMIE

The boredom of Eisenhower's position at Fort Sam Houston would not last long, at least on a personal level. A short time after he arrived there, he met a woman through some friends. Her name was Mamie Geneva Doud. She was attractive and had a personality that was the sheer opposite of Eisenhower's. While he was quiet and reserved, Mamie was boisterous and fun-loving. They also came from very different backgrounds. Eisenhower's family was solid working class, having clawed their way up from the days of near-poverty in the gloomy railroad town of Denison. Mamie, on the other hand, came from abundant wealth. Mamie's childhood

After Eisenhower graduated from West Point, the army stationed him at Fort Sam Houston, in San Antonio, Texas. There he met a cheerful and outgoing young woman named Mamie Geneva Doud.

was a world of mansions, servants, jewelry, and travel. Eisenhower had never known anyone like her back home.

Mamie was not particularly fond of Eisenhower at their first few meetings. Because Eisenhower was so serious about his work, he had a reputation around the base as someone who wasn't much interested in the company of women. Mamie may have taken this to mean he didn't think much of women overall. Whenever she was around, however, he was suddenly distracted and determined that they be together. He pestered her for a first date until he wore her down and she accepted. Then he worked hard to make a good impression—and not only on her. Knowing that her parents would be careful to judge him because he came from such humble beginnings, he used all of his powers of charm and persuasion to impress the Douds. His plan worked, for he was given permission to marry Mamie. They were engaged on Valentine's Day, 1916, and were married a few months later, on July 1.

Eisenhower and Mamie soon settled into a house on the base at Fort Sam Houston. Predictably, Mamie had some trouble adjusting to the life of an army wife. First of all, she was accustomed to living in great splendor, and the average second lieutenant's house on an army base was anything but splendorous. She tried to make up for this by sending for things from home, plus going out and buying new items, such as paintings, curtains, and furniture. Eisenhower apparently had no opinion on her redecorating efforts, as he seemed to feel that whatever made her happy made him happy as well. The fact that he wasn't around much probably helped, too. He very often had to be in his office early in the morning, and he didn't return home until late in the evening. Also, he might get a phone call telling him to report for duty at any hour of the day or night.

In spite of the differences in their background and personalities, Dwight and Mamie got married in 1916.

Mamie did not like the fact that her new husband was so busy, and she didn't hesitate to say so. Once, after they'd had an argument about it, Eisenhower gently took her aside and patiently explained that his duty and devotion to the army would always come first. While there's little doubt that Mamie wasn't too happy about this, she eventually accepted it.

A WAR ON THE OTHER SIDE OF THE WORLD

In Europe bloody fighting had been taking place for some time. World War I began in July 1914 following the June assassination of Franz Ferdinand, Austria-Hungary's archduke. Ferdinand's assassin, Gavrilo Princip, was thought to be a member of a terrorist organization connected to the Serbian government. Germany was also part of this organization because it was in a partnership with Austria-Hungary that collectively formed a group called the **Central Powers**. Their opponents at the start of the war, called the **Allied Powers**, included Russia, France, and Great Britain. In the weeks and months that followed, neighboring nations joined one side or the other.

America's president at the time, Woodrow Wilson, decided the nation's policy should be to remain neutral. Then, in early 1917, Germany launched a series of unprovoked submarine attacks against American vessels and also asked Mexico to became part of the Central Powers and attack the United States. Wilson responded by officially joining the Allies on April 6, 1917. American troops were sent to Europe a few months later, bringing manpower, equipment, and money.

As America's role in the war grew larger, America's army needed to grow along with it. That meant more soldiers and more training. Eisenhower went through a busy traveling period, where he was required to go from one base to another and ready troops for eventual service overseas. Mamie remained at Fort Sam Houston during this time, which meant they didn't see much of each other. Eisenhower nevertheless went about his duties with his

When the United States got involved in World War I in April 1917, Eisenhower was eager to take part in the fighting. The army, however, had other plans for him.

A Killer Even Greater Than the War Itself

The many fierce and bloody battles that characterized World War I were not the only cause of deaths for soldiers in 1918. That same year an outbreak of Spanish flu swept across the world, lasting well into 1919 and killing a minimum of 50 million people (with some estimates as high as twice that many)—considerably more casualties than the war itself. This caused enormous problems for Eisenhower while he was trying to help ready young recruits for the war, because young men were arriving already infected. Since there was no effective treatment, many of them died before their training had even begun.

usual diligence and devotion to getting things just right. He was also required to outfit and equip these young recruits, which meant he had to learn how to acquire things like helmets, rifles, and uniforms. Eisenhower received some valuable lessons in how the army worked—lessons that would pay off in the years ahead. Since he was a naturally friendly person and easy to get along with, he got most of the equipment he needed. The men who were training under him were also very fond of him, so they worked hard and usually turned into excellent soldiers.

The bad part about this training assignment was that Eisenhower desperately wanted to see some action in the war. But because he was such a good administrator, the army wanted to keep him right where he was. What saddened Eisenhower further was the fact that Mamie gave birth to their first child, a son named Doud Dwight, on September 24, 1917, while he was away.

If there was one consolation for Eisenhower during this period, it was the fact that he had been promoted several times. It was not unusual for promotions to come fast during wartime, and Eisenhower had managed to work his way up to the rank of major. Then, in 1918, he was promoted again—to lieutenant colonel—and along with this promotion came wonderful news. He was also being given a field command, leading troops into battle. There is little doubt that Eisenhower was thrilled by this, but on November 11, 1918, an **armistice** was signed to end World War I. Before Eisenhower even had a chance to take part in the fighting, it was over.

Camp Mead and Making Important Friends

Eisenhower's first big assignment after the war ended was to join a military convoy of trucks and other vehicles on a cross-country trip from the eastern side of the United States to the West Coast. The point of the mission was to judge the quality and readiness of America's roadways from a military standpoint. This was the age of transition from horse-pulled vehicles to those powered by gasoline engines. Today, such a journey would take a few days, perhaps a week. But back then the roads were not as smooth, nor were the vehicles as fast or reliable. The convoy left the East Coast in early July 1919 and didn't reach coastal California until two months later. Along the way the convoy encountered multiple vehicle breakdowns, bad weather, muddy roads, and dozens of other problems. But there were some bright spots, too. Eisenhower did get the chance to stop and see his wife and son for a time. Also, the soldiers who took part in this mission were often greeted in towns and cities as war heroes, with parties and parades.

After the cross-country trek Eisenhower and his family were moved to Camp Mead, in Maryland. There he was given more

Eisenhower reached the rank of lieutenant colonel during World War I. After the army discovered his administrative skills, he was given the task of acquiring equipment for soldiers heading overseas.

administrative duties. Since the war was over, the army was spending a lot of time downsizing. Many men were honorably discharged and sent back to civilian life. For Eisenhower this was a fairly quiet time. He helped to keep Camp Mead running, assisted the army in its efforts to thin out the forces, and managed to come home at a reasonable hour on most nights. He could finally spend time not just with his wife but with his beloved son. By all accounts, he was a good father; he liked to bring little Doud, whom he and Mamie had nicknamed Icky, around the base and show him off to his friends.

Eisenhower met famed general George S. Patton while both were stationed at Camp Mead, in Maryland. Sharing similar views on warfare, the two quickly became friends.

One of the other people stationed at Camp Mead—one who would not only play a huge role in Eisenhower's life but also in the future of America—was George Patton. Eisenhower's son, John, noted, "Adding to Patton's larger-than-life image in the Army was the fact that he was personally wealthy, and his wife was even wealthier. His consequent lack of need for his Army pay had exerted a considerable effect, no doubt, on his attitude. The Army was a hobby with Patton, though a mighty serious hobby." In spite of their different backgrounds, Patton and Eisenhower became good friends.

General Fox Conner was impressed by new ideas concerning the use of tanks from both Patton and Eisenhower. He was also impressed by Eisenhower as a person and would remember him years later.

The army had recently begun developing a new vehicle called the tank, which was basically a rolling artillery-shell launcher with a hard outer shell. Tanks could smash down trees and drive through shallow rivers, and they were very difficult for an enemy to destroy. Eisenhower and Patton agreed that tanks would play a large role in the future of warfare. But the army didn't necessarily agree with them, and when Eisenhower and Patton came up with some ideas on how tanks could be improved, the army didn't want to hear them. One person who did want to listen to their ideas, however, was a general named Fox Conner. Conner visited with Eisenhower and Patton at Camp Mead and listened patiently while they told him their ideas. General Conner left the meeting very impressed—not just with what he'd heard but with the general manner and attitude of Dwight Eisenhower.

Then tragedy struck. In January 1921 Eisenhower's beloved son, Doud, developed scarlet fever and died. Eisenhower and Mamie, who had been with their son until the end, were crushed. For weeks after it was all but impossible for them to go about their normal lives. A deeply depressed Eisenhower asked the army for a transfer so he could escape the horrible memories, but his request was denied. Then General Conner stepped in and helped. He gave Eisenhower an assignment in the Central American country of Panama. Eisenhower had never been to Panama, nor had he expressed any interest in going. But Conner was already stationed there and asked Eisenhower to join him. Ready for a fresh start after the death of Doud, he jumped at the chance. Not only would it be an interesting change, but he also knew he would learn a great deal from General Conner.

Mamie wasn't quite so excited about the idea of moving to Panama. She was even less excited when she got there to find their new home would be little more than a house on stilts on the edge of a tropical jungle. Her son John would later write, "It was not an inviting place, especially for Mamie, a young woman who was used to comfortable, if not luxurious, living, and who happened to be pregnant once again." At night she had to worry about everything from strange insects to bats and snakes. To make matters even more complicated, their second child, John, was born on August 3, 1922. Between the brutal Panamanian heat, the many things that crept and crawled, and the fact that there was nothing to do, Mamie eventually packed up her new baby and moved to her parents' upscale home in Denver. Eisenhower stayed behind to continue with his assignment.

Back to School

During this period Eisenhower and General Conner became close friends. Conner was, like Eisenhower, a fan of military history, having read even more on the subject than Eisenhower had. He loaned Eisenhower many of his books, then quizzed him on what he had learned. He would describe potential military situations, testing Eisenhower to see what he would do if he were in these situations. Clearly, he saw the potential for greatness in the young officer.

When Conner left Panama, Eisenhower wasn't sure what his next assignment would be. But then Conner stepped in again, arranging for Eisenhower to attend the General Command and Staff School in Leavenworth, Kansas. This military school literally handpicked the brightest young officers to attend—those they believed would go on to become their finest leaders.

Eisenhower had doubts about himself for the first time. He wondered if he was truly good enough to get through the school and graduate. As was the case at West Point, many never made it that far. The work was grueling, the hours long and hard. Eisenhower pushed himself to his very limits, absorbing all the information he could. Whenever he doubted himself, he would write a letter to General Conner. Conner wrote encouraging letters back, telling him he could be successful if he tried his best. Mamie also returned with their son, supporting Eisenhower in every way. When he graduated in 1926, he was first in his class. Many other important people in the army aside from Fox Conner were beginning to take notice.

IMPORTANT ASSIGNMENTS AT LAST

From the General Command and Staff School Eisenhower went to the Army War College, where he was further trained in warfare strategies and tactics. Again he did very well and graduated high in his class. After his graduation, he received a most exciting assignment—he was to go to Paris, France, to help put together a guidebook on the battlefields of World War I. His boss for this project would be General John J. "Black Jack" Pershing, perhaps the most recognized and famous American figure from World War I. Mamie was equally excited about the assignment, as she loved the idea of living in Europe.

Eisenhower suspected that the real purpose of his guidebook project was not just to make a detailed list of the World War I battlefields in France but to evaluate these same fields for a future war. Eisenhower took his Paris assignment as a hint that many of the higher-ups in the army were specifically training him, readying him for the next war. He certainly hoped so; if another war did break out, he didn't want to be spending all his time behind a desk again. Also, this was Eisenhower's first experience putting a book together, and it wasn't always easy. As an aide of his noted years later, "[Eisenhower] once had written [a book]. He said he struggled against a deadline and found himself still sending copy to the printer at the last minute. 'It's a whale of a job,' he said."

Following the Great War, Europe started on the long road to recovery. Some countries suffered greater hardships than others. Germany was one. The country barely had the resources needed to rebuild. After the war Germany was required to sign an agreement known as the **Treaty of Versailles**, which forced the nation to admit to causing the war in the first place. Germany also had to pay for much of the damage which amounted to billions of dollars. The treaty stripped the nation of land and colonial power in other countries and burdened it with economic **inflation** (unusually high prices on goods and services) the likes of which it had never seen. Germans wanted revenge.

One of the other duties Eisenhower had to perform while in France was to help General Pershing with administrative tasks. This included writing letters, memos, and speeches. Eisenhower also had to assist him in writing a book about his military experiences. This task presented Eisenhower with two problems: one, Pershing didn't write particularly well, and two, he was a notoriously difficult man to get along with. Nevertheless, Eisenhower threw himself into his job, tending to all of Pershing's needs and never complaining when Pershing became unpleasant. In time Pershing came to like Eisenhower very much, as did another important general—George C. Marshall. Marshall visited Pershing several times, and he wrote little notes to himself about how impressed he was with Eisenhower.

Eisenhower finished his Paris assignment in late 1929, and he and Mamie returned to the United States. Shortly thereafter the world was rocked by the greatest financial crisis in history, the **Great Depression**. In the 1920s there was a new and interesting way to buy goods and services—on credit. The idea was to buy now and pay later, but many spent more money than they really had. Also, people were overbuying stocks in the stock market—expecting their value to continue climbing and climb-

During the Great Depression communities like these "shantytowns" became common sights across America.

ing—which was impossible. On October 24, 1929—a date known as Black Thursday—the financial system collapsed. Less than a week later the value of American stocks had fallen to about half of their previous value. Since America's economy was so closely tied to the economies of other countries, the rest of the world soon found itself stuck in the same disastrous situation.

GETTING READY FOR WAR

One of the first jobs Eisenhower was given after his return to the States was to determine how ready the military was, the Great Depression notwithstanding, for another global war. Specifically, he had to find out how prepared American industries were to support the military in the event of such a conflict. Without factories making the most up-to-date bombs, tanks, guns, and missiles, American forces would be at a deep disadvantage during the heat of battle. Eisenhower dove into this assignment with his usual passion, and he eventually determined that American industries were nowhere close to being ready.

Most leaders in the army still didn't believe another war was imminent, but one who did was General Douglas MacArthur. A brilliant student and athlete at West Point, MacArthur was intelligent, motivated, and confident. He became an important figure in Eisenhower's life after he was appointed as the army chief of staff. This made MacArthur the army's highest-ranking officer, in charge of running its day-to-day affairs. MacArthur was impressed not only with Eisenhower's recommendations but also with Eisenhower himself. Eisenhower's plans were put into action, and MacArthur kept Eisenhower as an aide.

Eisenhower was now on the cutting edge of the U.S. Army. He was becoming friends with many of the most powerful

General Douglas MacArthur possessed a magnificent military mind, but was also known for a giant ego and little patience for anyone who disagreed with him. He had a particular fondness for Eisenhower and put him on his staff as an aide.

people, and his ideas were being used to reform and reshape the military in preparation for whatever challenges lay ahead. The downside for him, at least on a personal level, was that General MacArthur could be a very difficult person to work with. He kept strange hours—often getting up in the middle of the night and expecting his staff to be there for him—hated when anyone disagreed with him, and thought of himself as godlike. Still, he was very fond of Eisenhower (Eisenhower was smart and went out of his way not to irritate MacArthur) and was happy to act as his mentor and teacher.

In Germany a frustrated public began listening to the rising political leader Adolf Hitler. Hitler was a member of the **Nazi Party**. He knew the pains of the Great Depression would lead people to favor and support the Nazis. As one man stated in William Sheridan Allen's *The Nazi Seizure of Power: The Experience of a Single German Town, 1930–1935*, "Most of those who joined the Nazis did so because they wanted a radical answer to the economic problem. Then, too, people wanted a hard, sharp, clear leadership." Hitler became the nation's chancellor in 1933, having successfully eliminated all other political parties. He ignored the Treaty of Versailles and began rebuilding Germany's military.

Around the same time Japan was hoping to expand its own power in eastern Asia. Japan had fought on the side of the Allies in World War I and, as a result, had gained a great deal of land, resources, and political influence. But the Japanese hungered for more, and they set their sights on weaker nations that were close by. The Japanese military invaded and occupied nearby Manchuria (most of which lies within northeastern China) in 1931. Their ultimate plan was to conquer China altogether.

When MacArthur was assigned to be chief military adviser in the Philippines in 1935, he took Eisenhower along with him.

Adolf Hitler led the Nazi Party to great heights of power in Germany following World War I and began a ruthless quest to conquer Europe.

Mamie, remembering the misery of Panama, chose not to go along. Eisenhower surveyed the Philippines in order to report how well it could defend itself in the event of a wartime attack. Eisenhower also learned how to fly an airplane during this time. Still, he craved the opportunity to do more for the army, to make a more significant contribution before America got into the war overseas.

Then he caught a break. In the spring of 1939 General George C. Marshall became the army's new chief of staff. He remembered Eisenhower from his visit with Black Jack Pershing, and he decided to assign Eisenhower to a base named Fort Lewis, near Seattle, Washington. Marshall knew as well as anyone that U.S. forces were going to play a role in World War II. In later years Eisenhower would come to admire Marshall tremendously. When he wrote about the American military's readiness for the upcoming war, he said of Marshall, "This was due to the vision and determination of one man, General Marshall. [He was] determined that at whatever cost to himself or to anyone else the Army should be decently prepared for the conflict."

FROM WAR HERO TO PRESIDENT

$\mathcal{B}$y 1941 Germany, Italy, and Japan had created a partnership to help fulfill their joint ambitions. These three nations, along with Bulgaria, Hungary, and Romania, became known as the Axis Powers. Those fighting against them (a group that would eventually constitute nearly fifty countries) were, just as in World War I, called the Allied Powers. World War II was fought in two main theaters—the European theater, where Germany was looking to expand its empire, and the Pacific theater, where Japan hoped to do the same.

PREPARATIONS CONTINUE

Back in the United States Eisenhower continued to prepare the army for the potential conflict in Europe. He was promoted to the rank of colonel and was assigned to work under General Walter Krueger. Krueger was tough, direct, and sometimes mean-spirited, but he was also deeply respected. In August 1941 Eisenhower began helping General Krueger to train and supply nearly a quarter of a million soldiers based in the southern half of the United States, from New Mexico to Florida. To make sure he was centrally located, Eisenhower was assigned to a base in San Antonio, Texas. This time he and Mamie were given a beautiful home complete with servants, all paid for by the army. It meant little to Eisenhower personally, since he was not there much, but Mamie could not have been happier.

Once all the new soldiers were trained, outfitted, and given the supplies and equipment they required, they needed to be tested. This meant they had to undergo a series of military exercises in order to evaluate their readiness for war. These exercises also gave army leaders a chance to evaluate many of their weapons and vehicles as well. They were held in northern Louisiana, and thus they became known as the Louisiana Maneuvers. They took place from August to September 1941 and involved more than half a million men. The men were divided into two groups that had to engage in simulated battles.

Eisenhower played a key role in deciding strategies and tactics for the men on his side, and they were eventually declared the winners. He was praised for his superb leadership, with reporters from both public and military newspapers swarming around him. Eisenhower did not care for all the fuss and attention, but he was happy his side had done so well. He would later comment that the Louisiana Maneuvers also gave the army a chance to eliminate all soldiers—both officers and enlisted men—who were not up to the demands and challenges of real fighting. Eisenhower's excellent performance earned him a most treasured prize—promotion from colonel to one-star general.

THE UNITED STATES ENTERS WORLD WAR II

Franklin Delano Roosevelt was the president at the start of America's involvement in World War II. Prior to this he wanted to keep America out of the actual fighting. He did, however, sell war supplies to Allied nations shortly after Hitler invaded Poland.

When Japan decided to invade the nearby nations of Thailand and the Philippines, it knew it first had to strike at America's naval forces stationed in nearby Pearl Harbor in Hawaii.

Eisenhower and other military leaders prepared for U.S. participation and readiness for war in the Louisiana Maneuvers.

On December 7, 1941, more than 350 Japanese planes carried out a surprise attack on the Pearl Harbor base. Even Eisenhower was shocked by their actions: "I was certain that the United States would be drawn into the whirlpool of the war, but I was mistaken as to the manner of our entry. I assumed that Japan would make no move against us until after we were committed to the European war." Nearly 2,500 American soldiers and citizens were killed in the Pearl Harbor massacre. Nine ships sank, and more than twenty others were heavily damaged. In response Roosevelt asked **Congress** to declare war on Japan the very next day, which it did.

The Japanese bombing of an American naval base in Pearl Harbor on December 7, 1941, drove the United States to formally enter World War II.

With America officially involved in World War II, General Marshall decided some key changes needed to be made to the overall structure of the military. He wanted it to be more stream-lined, able to act and move more quickly. To help with this project, he chose Eisenhower to be his second in command.

As the deputy to the army's chief of staff, Eisenhower would have tremendous power and influence; it was the opportunity of a lifetime. But Eisenhower wasn't the least bit happy about it. Since becoming a general, he thought he would, at last, be sent into battle. Instead, he watched helplessly as many of his friends, such as George Patton, were given command of actual troops. Eisenhower went about assisting General Marshall in the best way he could, but Marshall soon realized that Eisenhower wasn't happy. In a rare moment of kindness Marshall wrote a letter to President Roosevelt recommending that Eisenhower be more involved in assigning troops to the most critical battlefields—and that he be promoted again. Roosevelt honored this request, and Eisenhower became a two-star general.

Eisenhower's new job was one of massive importance: he had to study the war's overall scope and make recommendations on how American forces would best be used. Put simply, Eisenhower had to plan what the American military would do in World War II. After thorough study and consideration, using all of his intelligence and experience, he decided that, in spite of the attacks by the Japanese on Pearl Harbor, the U.S. military should focus first on the fighting in the European theater and worry about the Pacific theater later on. He felt that the most important battles would be fought in Europe and that the best chance for victory lay in fending off the Nazis rather than the Japanese.

A Commander at Last

General Marshall and President Roosevelt carefully reviewed Eisenhower's plans, then agreed to follow them; Eisenhower had just created the blueprint for America's participation in World War II. As a reward for his excellent work, Marshall then gave Eisenhower what he wanted most—a command in the field. Starting in June 1942, Eisenhower was to be in charge of all American forces in Europe. This would not put him on the field of battle per se, but he would be making the important decisions concerning strategy and tactics. This meant he was about to send thousands of young men into harm's way, knowing many would never return alive. But he had been preparing for this job all his life, and he was ready for it.

Now promoted to three-star general, Eisenhower moved to London and into his new command headquarters. He first planned to launch an assault on Nazi forces in a few European locations during spring 1943. However, he was told that Nazi forces needed to be driven out of Africa instead. Eisenhower again designed a plan, and he was given command not only of American troops but British troops as well. Eisenhower knew he would have a tough time. He also knew that succeeding with the Africa plan would not mean the end of the war, but it would be an important part of achieving this goal. As he stated in his book *Crusade in Europe*, "The African venture was looked upon as diversionary in character but necessitated by the circumstances of the moment and in the hope that from it we would achieve great results."

The battles were long and hard, with many deaths and injuries on both sides. Since this was Eisenhower's first command in the field, he made some mistakes. But he learned from each one

After creating most of the military plans for World War II, Eisenhower was given command of American forces in Europe in June 1942. He was also promoted to lieutenant general.

Eisenhower was responsible for much of the Allied invasion of Normandy, known as Operation Overlord, with the goal of driving the Nazis out of France.

and was certain not to make them twice. For a time it seemed as though both sides were holding their ground. Then, in the late spring, American and British forces began to gain the upper hand. By early summer nearly all Nazi troops had been pushed out of Africa, and Eisenhower had achieved his objective. In July 1943, as a four-star general, Eisenhower received similar orders—to remove all Nazis from the Italian island of Sicily. He did so with the same masterful efficiency, and the following September his troops reached the Italian mainland. Not long afterward, Italian dictator and Hitler's ally Benito Mussolini left office, to Eisenhower's delight. As one of Eisenhower's aides noted, "Before breakfast Ike received a message relayed from Algiers that Mussolini had quit. . . . This was extraordinarily good news."

By early 1944 Eisenhower and the rest of the Allied commanders decided that the best way to put an end to the war was to first invade the Nazi-occupied nation of France, then continue into Germany itself. For the first part of this plan to work, the Allies had to land on the beaches of Normandy, located along the country's northern coast and heavily protected by Nazis troops. Eisenhower, along with everyone else at the command level, knew this would probably be the all-or-nothing battle of the war. If the Allied forces failed, the war could stretch on for many more months or even years. If they succeeded, however, they could defeat the Nazis and put an end to the conflict.

OPERATION OVERLORD

Eisenhower was put in charge of planning the invasion. It was called Operation Overlord, and it was, without a doubt, the most important moment of his career. The amount of preparation he did was unprecedented. He studied maps and intelligence reports, gathered opinions from other generals as well as anyone who had been in the region and knew it well, and ordered the bombing of miles of railroads so that the Nazis would not be able to send in more supplies and soldiers. The other challenge for Eisenhower was to make sure that Operation Overlord was kept a secret, and so he shared the plan only with a small group of his most trusted friends and advisers.

The Nazis knew that a major attack of some kind was coming, but they weren't sure where it would occur. They believed Eisenhower was going to attack the seaport of Calais, which was farther east along the French coast, largely because it was closer to England and therefore easier for Eisenhower's forces to reach. But Eisenhower knew the value of surprise. He prepared hundreds of planes and ships, as well as more than 150,000 men. He also took the time to visit with many of the men before Operation Overlord began, knowing that a visit from their commander would heighten their spirits and their motivation. As Captain Harry Butcher, Eisenhower's aide at the time, noted in his book *My Three Years with Eisenhower: The Personal Diary of Captain Harry C. Butcher*, "Ike wandered through them, stepping over packs, guns, and a variety of equipment such as only paratroop people can devise, chinning [talking] with this and that one. All were put at ease."

Operation Overlord began early in the morning on June 6. Under cover of darkness men began parachuting from airplanes. Then, as sunlight broke, ships landed on the beaches to drop off thousands of soldiers. By that night Allied forces numbered more than 175,000. The fighting was fierce and bloody, with thousands of deaths on both sides.

The Nazis also knew how important this battle would be, and they had no intention of giving up. The Allied push lasted for nearly two months, and there were times when it seemed as though failure was imminent. Then the Allies broke through German lines in the town of Saint-Lô, and Eisenhower's old friend George Patton rolled through with hundreds of his tanks. By the end of August the Nazis had been driven out of the French capital of Paris. By September they had lost their grip on the rest of France as well. Even though Operation Overlord had cost the Allies dearly in terms of human life, it had been a success.

Eisenhower could not have been more pleased. Since his name was attached to the success at Normandy, many began regarding him as one of the greatest heroes of World War II. Even the army felt he should be rewarded for his brilliance, and they promoted him in December 1944 to the highest possible rank—the five-star General of the Army. Eisenhower received all of the praise and accolades with his usual modesty, but he was no doubt happier about the Allied victory than anything else. However, he knew that the war was still not over.

Allied troops landing on Utah Beach during the start of Operation Overlord, June 6, 1944.

The very day after he received his promotion, the Nazis broke through Allied lines in Belgium in a last-ditch attempt to gain a good position and, just maybe, win the war. But the Allies had no intention of letting this final Nazi push go any farther. Eisenhower let Patton loose again, and Patton's tanks met the Nazi forces head-on. More blood was spilled, and hundreds more lives were lost, but eventually the Allies broke up the Nazi attack. In doing so they also broke the Nazis' spirit. Nazi losses were now mounting all over Europe as well as in the Soviet Union, where Soviet forces were responsible for heavy Nazi casualties. Germany had lost millions of men and was running out of supplies.

The final blow came when Soviet soldiers, following a plan that Eisenhower had helped to design, crossed into the German capital city of Berlin, where Hitler was hiding in his underground bunker. The war there turned into a street fight, with Soviets and Nazis often battling in hand-to-hand combat. Sadly, with so many professional soldiers dead, Nazi leaders forced children— none of whom knew anything about warfare—to pick up guns and knives and continue the resistance. As a result thousands of youngsters were killed. As a final act of cowardice Adolf Hitler committed suicide on April 30, 1945, when he was told that Soviet tanks were just a few blocks from his underground hide-out. He knew they would capture him, imprison him, put him on trial, and then, most likely, execute him.

Knowing that the war was lost, the Nazis surrendered a week later, on May 7. Alfred Jodl, the chief of staff of the Nazi forces, met with Eisenhower and his staff in Rheims, France, and signed the official documents, which ordered Nazi forces to cease further hostilities everywhere.

IKE MAKES SURE HISTORY IS RECORDED

The end of hostilities in the European theater also meant the liberation of countless labor and concentration camps. These camps were nestled in quiet wooded areas of Germany, and neighboring countries, where prisoners, mostly Jewish, were massacred by the millions. In mid–April 1945, Eisenhower toured one of these camps to see the horrors for himself. There he found piles of dead bodies stacked in sheds awaiting cremation, ghastly torture chambers, and huge mass graves. Infuriated, he ordered that journalists be permitted to tour the camp in order for records—ranging from detailed articles to photos and movies—to be made so that the world would know exactly what had happened. He also made German citizens walk through the camps for the same reason. Eisenhower wanted to be certain that no one, either then or in the future, would be able to claim that the Holocaust never really took place.

The Nazi surrender did not mean that World War II was over—the Japanese were still fighting the Allies in the Pacific theater. The Allies were making good progress, but that didn't stop the Japanese from fighting on. They hoped to make the battles so bloody and costly that the Allies would consider a peace settlement. Concerned that an extended war would cost hundreds of thousands more lives, President Harry S. Truman (who had been Roosevelt's vice president and therefore succeeded him when Roosevelt died on April 12) authorized atomic bombs—which the United States had only recently developed—to be dropped on Japanese cities. One was dropped on Hiroshima (on August 6), the second on Nagasaki (on August 9). The destruction that resulted was unprecedented and enormous. Japan then had no choice but to surrender, which it did on August 14, with the formal surrender following on September 2. Finally, World War II was over.

A HERO'S WELCOME

Dwight Eisenhower was regarded by many as the greatest figure of World War II; a hero not just in America but in free nations everywhere. After the fighting ended, he went on a tour of various countries, where he was treated like royalty and showered with gifts and good wishes. When he returned to the United States, the adulation was even greater. From the moment he stepped off the plane, cameras flashed, and crowds of thousands cheered and whistled. He rode in the back of limousines in parade after parade, then attended dinners and other ceremonies in his honor. One of Eisenhower's aides noted that the Pentagon was "crowded with cheering men and women of the War Department. . . . Ike responded warmly, praising their part in the great teamwork that had won the war." He also got to be with Mamie

Eisenhower was given a hero's welcome wherever he went in the weeks and months following the end of World War II.

for the first time since January 1944. Not long after, he had to return to Europe. He was asked to command the Allied troops that remained in Europe—now that they had won the war, they had to win the peace by stabilizing the area—plus oversee the management of all Nazi prisoners.

Once this task was completed, Eisenhower was given a new title—army chief of staff. It was the same job held by two others with whom Eisenhower had worked years earlier—Generals Douglas MacArthur and George Marshall. But his duties would be a bit different from theirs. His job was not to build up the U.S. Army but to reduce it. It was a massive project, getting troops out of Europe and sending them back home, then deciding who would be discharged from the military and who would not. Over the next three years Eisenhower shrunk the size of American forces from 8 million to less than one million. In 1948 he left active duty and announced his retirement.

Eisenhower was still enormously popular with the American people when he left the army. They knew him well as a likable individual, a war hero, a brilliant strategist, and a great patriot. It wasn't long before both major political parties—**Democratic** and **Republican**—began to realize the value of this popularity. At the end of 1948 there would be a presidential election. And the leaders of both parties thought that Eisenhower would be a perfect candidate. But would he be interested in taking on a new career?

In spite of the fact that Eisenhower was asked by both sides if he would accept their presidential nomination, he refused. Instead, he focused his attention on writing a book about his experiences in the war. It was called *Crusade in Europe* and went on to become not only a best seller but also one of the most widely praised military memoirs in history. Then he accepted a presidency of a different sort—of Columbia University. Located in New York City, Columbia is a member of the Ivy League, and one of the best schools in the nation. Columbia wanted to make use of Eisenhower's superb managerial and administrative skills. Although the environment and structure were very different from what Eisenhower had known as a general, he eventually settled into the position and began making positive changes.

Eisenhower was offered, and accepted, the presidency of Columbia University, in New York, in 1948.

He improved the school's financial situation, and during his tenure the university hired some of the best professors available. He and Mamie also bought their first home (all of their previous homes were the property of the army) in Gettysburg, Pennsylvania.

A NEW THREAT

Toward the end of 1950 Eisenhower left his position at Columbia because President Truman asked him to return to military duty and take charge of all **NATO** forces. The greatest concern of the NATO allies was the Soviet Union. Following the end of World War II the Soviets began overseeing the governments of several European regions under Joseph Stalin's regime. Stalin

After World War II, American leaders feared that Stalin might try to invade war-torn Europe in its weakened state.

believed in the political philosophy of **communism**. This was the opposite of America's philosophy of **capitalism**.

Even though America fought alongside the Soviets in World War II, there existed a distrustful relationship between them. This tension created a situation of mutual suspicion that became known as the **cold war**. President Truman was concerned that Stalin would try to exploit the weaknesses of war-torn Europe—for example, he might try to conquer much of it. It would be his way of securing his own power as well as spreading communism. Forming NATO was a way of getting many anticommunist nations together to deter any such attempt on Stalin's part—and Eisenhower's job was to run the army that would do this. The problem was, most of Europe was still trying to rebuild after the destruction of World War II. Furthermore, in 1950 a new conflict was developing in the small Asian nation of Korea.

Korea had been occupied by both American and Soviet forces during World War II. When the war was over, neither side could agree on who would govern Korea. In the end, the nation became divided into two parts, north and south. Russia's communist leadership would oversee North Korea, and America's democratic leadership would control South Korea. Then, in June 1950, North Korean forces attacked South Korea because its communist leadership wanted to control both halves.

The Korean War was raging by autumn 1950, and the spread of communism was considered a huge and looming threat. By 1951 no progress had been made toward ending the conflict, either militarily or through negotiation. As a result, many Americans were ready for a change in the White House.

I Like Ike

Eisenhower retired from his NATO position in May 1952. The Republican Party asked again if he would consider running for office. Eisenhower's popularity was still as strong as ever, and the Republicans were desperate to get back some political power. Between the presidencies of Franklin D. Roosevelt and Harry Truman, a Democrat had been in the White House since March 1933, a span of almost twenty years. If Eisenhower would run, the Republicans believed they had a chance of finally having one of their own as the president again.

The problem was, not all Republicans wanted Eisenhower. The leading Republican candidate up to that point had been Ohio senator Robert Taft. His father, William Howard Taft, had been the twenty-seventh president as well as the tenth chief justice of the Supreme Court. Taft had many powerful friends and connections, and he wasn't about to stand aside for Eisenhower without a fight.

Eisenhower decided to give the presidency a try this time. He didn't think either Truman or Taft would do a very good job. He believed that many of Truman's domestic policies—those that concern the governing of America itself—were going in the wrong direction. And he thought that Taft's ideas about foreign policy—America's position in relation to other countries—were foolish and dangerous.

After months of bitter fighting, the Republicans finally decided to put their support behind Eisenhower. They made the decision in July 1952 at the Republican National Convention in Chicago. Harry Truman had already announced that he would

The Republican Party asked Eisenhower to be their presidential candidate in 1952.

not run for the presidency again. The Democratic Party chose Illinois governor Adlai Stevenson to run in Truman's place.

Over the next few months Eisenhower hammered away at both Stevenson and the Democratic Party overall. He blamed them for not doing more to squelch the spread of communism around the world and for the ongoing troubles in Korea—which he promised to resolve.

Eisenhower's popularity was so overwhelming that the push to make him president became known as the "I Like Ike" campaign. Between his war record and his likable personality, he was seen as a great American. When election day came around—November 4, 1952—Eisenhower received 34 million votes to Stevenson's 27 million, winning thirty-nine of the forty-eight states. Republicans also won majorities in both houses of Congress—the **Senate** and the **House of Representatives**. It was a landslide to say the least and the beginning of a new chapter in American political history. The humble, hardworking boy from Abilene, Kansas, was headed to the White House.

Eisenhower beat Democratic opponent Adlai Stevenson in a landslide victory in November 1952 becoming the thirty-fourth president of the United States.

FIRST TERM AS PRESIDENT (1953–1957)

Four

$\mathcal{D}$wight Eisenhower entered into the presidency with mixed feelings. There is no doubt that he believed he was the best person for the job, and that he had done a service to the country by keeping both Taft and Truman out of the White House. It is likely he looked forward to the presidency as a new challenge; if nothing else, Eisenhower certainly loved a challenge. But there were also times when he clearly was not enjoying himself. He went through periods when he would never miss an opportunity to get out of the Oval Office, and even out of Washington altogether. He once bitterly referred to the presidency as a pressure cooker, and unfriendly reporters delighted in taking pictures of him playing golf on the putting green that he had built on the White House grounds. The impression they were trying to create was of Eisenhower as a do-nothing president; that is, that little of importance occurred during his presidency and therefore he had little to do. In truth, Eisenhower dealt with some of the most difficult issues in U.S. history, and by all accounts he handled them with a dedication to fairness, decency, and common sense.

THE COLD WAR

If there was one central issue that loomed over Eisenhower's presidency from beginning to end, it was the cold war. The majority of Americans understood the cold war in one word—communism. Communism came to represent everything that threatened the goodness and benefits of the American way of life after World War II. Americans believed that the government of the Soviet Union, led by Joseph Stalin, wanted to conquer the world and destroy the United States.

Eisenhower seemed to agree. In January 1953 he wrote, "We must show the wickedness of purpose in the communist promises and convince dependent peoples that their only hope of maintaining independence, once attained, is through the cooperation with the free world." He viewed communism as a kind of poison, one that had to be neutralized before it spread throughout the whole body of the world and killed it. However, he also knew that most nations were not eager for another long and bloody conflict. So he decided to approach the communist threat with a policy created during the Truman administration known as **containment**—stopping communist influence from spreading rather than attacking it at its core. Eisenhower knew that there were communist leaders in parts of Europe and Asia; his goal was not to destroy them but to keep them from gaining any more power than they already had.

The Korean War

Eisenhower knew it would be impossible to achieve this without some degree of military conflict, and one of the biggest was the battle in Korea that had begun before he was president. He had promised to deal with it during his campaign, and he had every intention of keeping that promise. Although some still called it a mere police action, Eisenhower knew a war when he saw one.

By the time he reached the presidency, the Korean War had caused thousands of deaths, cost billions of dollars, and resolved nothing; neither side seemed to be gaining on the other. Many of

Eisenhower's advisers urged him to send more soldiers and weaponry so that South Korea would have the might to crush its northern enemies. But Eisenhower wanted to end the fighting quickly and peacefully. By spring 1953, with Stalin then dead, the North Korean leadership agreed to an armistice, and a cease-fire was ordered on July 27. Eisenhower was relieved that the conflict did not escalate to the point where the United States might have

One of the most important issues Eisenhower had to deal with in his first term involved hostilities between North and South Korea.

A War That Never Really Ended

In spite of the July 27 cease-fire agreement, the Korean War has never formally ended. In fact, many still consider it to be an active war, despite the absence of actual fighting. Hostile relations between North Korea and many of the nations it fought more than half a century ago persist, perhaps the most volatile being between North Korean and South Korean forces, plus the United States. Immediately following the cease-fire North Korea as a nation did fairly well from an economic standpoint. But over time its economy has dwindled to almost nothing, and most of its citizens live in abject poverty. South Korea, on the other hand, struggled at first but today does fairly well. The strip of land that separates the two countries is known as the Demilitarized Zone and is guarded by soldiers on both sides, as well as being carpeted with thousands of land mines. While some peace proposals have been offered to North Korea, its leaders have consistently refused to make any substantial moves in that direction. In fact, North Korea has become increasingly aggressive toward its enemies around the world. It actively seeks the development of nuclear weapons and regularly makes threats to use them. It also keeps tight control of its citizens, rarely permitting them any modern freedoms, such as Internet access or exposure to news media, that do not originate from the government.

to once again make use of the atomic bomb. In April 1954 he wrote in his presidential diary, "The power of the bomb is not of itself a threat to us or to others. The danger arises from the existence."

VIETNAM

Another example of communist political and military aggression that Eisenhower would have to address during his presidency occurred in the Asian nation of Vietnam. Before World War II Vietnam was a colony of the French government. After the war it was occupied and controlled by the Japanese. When Japan surrendered in 1945, French leaders assumed Vietnam would submit to their control again. However, there was a political activist in northern Vietnam named Ho Chi Minh who had different ideas. Minh was a communist, and he wanted his nation to be independent. To reach this goal, he formed a government and an army.

French military forces, with help from America as well as Vietnamese people who were against communism, tried to remove Minh from power. But Minh's forces proved tougher than anyone expected. In 1954, with neither side having won a clear victory, it was decided that Vietnam would be temporarily divided in two, with the idea that there would be a presidential election in 1956. Whoever won this election would be the leader of all of Vietnam, and the country would be united again.

North Vietnam was ruled by Minh, and South Vietnam was ruled by its prime minister, Ngo Dinh Diem. Eisenhower was comfortable with Diem. Diem was opposed to communism and willing to let America have some influence over him. The United States was also giving him money, military equipment, and training for his armies. However, the election that many hoped would stabilize the region never took place, and armed conflict continued in Vietnam, becoming particularly intense toward the end of Eisenhower's time in the White House. Ultimately, the American military would become involved in a full-scale war with North Vietnamese forces, but this would not occur until after Eisenhower's presidency.

THE GENEVA SUMMIT—A NEW BEGINNING?

In March 1953 communist leader Joseph Stalin died. In the aftermath Eisenhower hoped Stalin's successor would be interested in starting a new—and, he hoped, more positive—chapter in American-Soviet relations. To that end he invited the key figures in the Soviet government to meet and discuss the future. They accepted his offer, and the meeting was scheduled for July 1955 in the Swiss capital city of Geneva. Also in attendance would be the leaders of both France and Great Britain.

On the Soviet side three delegates came: Nikolai Bulganin, the minister of defense; Georgy Zhukov, a decorated military leader of the Soviet army during World War II; and Nikita Khrushchev, who oversaw military actions during World War II and at that time was a professional politician. Eisenhower already knew Zhukov and had great respect and fondness for him. Eisenhower hoped that Zhukov would be acting as the leader of the group, since they had such a good relationship. But he quickly realized it was Khrushchev who held not only the most power among the three but would probably be Stalin's replacement as well.

Both sides had ideas about the future. But they had difficulty agreeing on anything, and the meeting seemed to be going nowhere. Then Eisenhower suggested a plan called Open Skies. In short, it would be an agreement by which each side had open access to the other's military establishments. For example, each side would be able to fly planes over the other's bases, along specific routes and at prearranged times, and take photographs of the weapons, vehicles, and equipment that the other side was developing. Eisenhower said that this plan would foster a greater trust between everyone, because no one would be able to secretly develop weapons of mass destruction (weapons with the sole purpose of obliteration, which would surely lead to a World War III scenario and cause the deaths of millions).

Following the death of Joseph Stalin in March 1953, former Stalin adviser Nikita Khrushchev took over as the Soviet leader. Eisenhower hoped to forge better relationships between their two nations now that Khrushchev was in charge, but it was not to be.

The British and French leaders thought that Open Skies was an excellent idea, but Khrushchev rejected it immediately. As Eisenhower biographer Stephen Ambrose noted, "Khrushchev said the idea was nothing more than a bald espionage plot against the Soviet Union." Krushchev was convinced that Eisenhower's goal was to expose the Soviet Union's military weaknesses, which could then be easily exploited and give the United States a huge military advantage. Knowing that America's nuclear weapons were far more advanced than the Soviets', Khrushchev saw the Open Skies plan as a way for America to retrieve the last piece of the puzzle they needed to destroy the Soviet Union—it would know exactly where to target its bombs. At the end of the summit Khrushchev left in a huff, more convinced than ever that the United States and its allies were out to betray the Soviets. Nevertheless, there was a general feeling of hopefulness that, at least, Soviet and American leaders had met and sat down to discuss key issues; something they hadn't done in a decade.

CRISIS IN THE SUEZ CANAL

Late in Eisenhower's first term as president he found himself confronted with a very difficult foreign-affairs problem. In 1956 Egypt was ruled by Colonel Gamal Abdel Nasser, a former leader of the Egyptian Revolution before becoming the nation's president. Nasser had a rocky relationship with Great Britain and France. Prior to World War II Egypt was heavily under French and British control, but Nasser wanted to establish Egypt as a free and independent country once the war was over.

One of Nasser's pet projects was to build a dam on the Nile River in the city of Aswan as part of a larger plan to modernize Egypt.

Great Britain, France, and the United States, in an attempt to improve the frosty relationship, agreed to help pay for the construction of the dam. Then it was discovered that Nasser was buying weapons from Czechoslovakia, which, at the time, was under communist control. Great Britain, France, and the United States immediately pulled out of the dam project.

Annoyed, Nasser then turned to the Soviet Union for the money. He also decided to nationalize the existing Suez Canal, which the British had built and which was one of their crucial commercial waterways. In response British and French leaders came up with a plan: they asked Israel to invade Egypt. Then British and French forces would enter Egypt under the pretense that they were helping to stop the Israeli invasion. Once they were there, they could regain control of the Suez Canal.

When Eisenhower heard about the plan—which he did only after it had been launched—he was furious. He did not see it so much as an attempt to get back control of the Suez Canal but as the petty actions of two colonial powers who were angry because one of the nations they used to govern was trying to break free of their grip. Eisenhower insisted that Great Britain, France, and Israel immediately withdraw their troops from Egypt. Because the United States was so powerful, they had no choice but to obey. Then a new problem arose: when the governments of Great Britain and France stopped managing Egypt's affairs (for better or worse), the region became unstable. Great Britain and France also lost their colonial control over several other nations in the area following World War II, resulting in a great amount of conflict and many power struggles that would last for decades to come.

Joseph McCarthy

For the most part, Eisenhower was a foreign-affairs president, meaning he spent more of his time and attention on global issues than on those occurring within America's borders. This is not to say he wasn't interested in any of the problems at home, but rather that America was enjoying a period of unprecedented prosperity and growth. Eisenhower was never one to fix something that wasn't broken, so he was content to sit back and let things be. Still, there were a few matters that required his attention.

One of the most alarming domestic problems that found its way to Eisenhower's desk had to do with Joseph McCarthy, a Wisconsin senator. His first few years in Washington were largely unremarkable and undistinguished. He was not very popular with his fellow senators, as he was a heavy drinker and had a loud, combative personality.

In February 1950 he made a speech in which he claimed to have a list of more than two hundred people working in the **State Department** (the agency of the U.S. government that deals with matters concerning foreign countries) who were known communists. McCarthy's claim naturally frightened most American citizens. He even went so far as to hint that Harry Truman, the president at the time, was happy to let these "commies," as he called them, infiltrate the government, thus gaining control of America from the inside. History professor Ellen Schrecker noted in her book *The Age of McCarthyism*, "By the summer of 1946, the White House was under considerable pressure to eliminate politically undesirable employees. . . . At the end of November, Truman set up a special interagency commission to handle the job."

McCarthy was at the height of his reign of terror when Eisenhower became president. In spite of urgings from his supporters, Eisenhower had no intention of facing McCarthy directly. Eisenhower predicted that McCarthy would eventually pursue the wrong person and become discredited. He was right—in autumn 1953 McCarthy attacked a beloved World War II general named Ralph W. Zwicker. In public hearings McCarthy said that Zwicker had the mind of a child and was unfit to serve in the army. Zwicker and his attorney handled these hearings perfectly; they both acted in a calm, respectable manner, and in time the public began to see McCarthy for what he really was—bitter, bloodthirsty, and desperate for attention. In early December 1954 McCarthy was **censured**—formally condemned for his actions—by the Senate, and his influence on the American public as well as within the government evaporated. To this day the word **McCarthyism** remains part of the English language; it refers to the act of accusing someone, or a group of people, of disloyalty without the necessary proof.

Taking It on the Road

One of Eisenhower's proudest domestic accomplishments during his first term was the launch of a long-discussed plan to build thousands of miles of highways. Eisenhower felt that America needed more reliable roadways from coast to coast, not just for the purpose of private and commercial travel but also to facilitate military operations in the event that America experienced warfare on its own soil. The idea of expanding the nation's roads had been brought up during Franklin D. Roosevelt's administration, but there were several hurdles that Roosevelt could not overcome—not least of which was the fact that most of America's money was being poured into the war effort.

Eisenhower revisited the plan during the last year of his first term. Once the routes were established, he signed the Federal Aid Highway Act of 1956, which called for $25 billion to be spent over two decades in order to build more than 41,000 miles of roads. Eisenhower was inspired to pursue this plan, at least in part, by his difficult experiences with the cross-country military convoy in 1919, and also from the German Autobahn, which he learned of during World War II. Back then there was only one road that reached from coast to coast, and it was in terrible shape in certain areas. Eisenhower knew this was dangerous in terms of national defense and readiness. Also, building more roadways would open up new opportunities for American business as well as vacationers; it would be easier to visit friends and relatives, and people could easily drive to parts of the country they had never seen before.

Health Problems and a Second Term

In September 1955 Eisenhower had the first major health scare of his life. While on vacation with Mamie in the Rocky Mountains of Colorado, he awoke in the middle of the night with severe chest pains. There had been no indication of illness earlier in the day—he had played golf, visited with friends, wrote some letters, and seemed cheerful and upbeat. When the pains came, he asked Mamie for some milk of magnesia, an over-the-counter medicine used to treat an upset stomach.

Mamie found this request strange, as Eisenhower rarely used medicine of any kind. She called for his doctor, who came in the middle of the night and told Eisenhower to get some more rest. Eisenhower slept late the next day—which was very unusual for him—and the doctor then recommended that he be brought to the hospital. As it turned out, Eisenhower had had a heart attack. He was ordered to remain in bed for more rest.

THE EISENHOWERS IN THE WHITE HOUSE

Since Eisenhower had spent his adult life as a solider, he was accustomed to a carefully structured schedule every day. When he became president, he saw no reason to change. He was up every day at 6:00 a.m. and at his desk no later than 8:00 a.m. He would work on the day's problems until early in the afternoon usually eating lunch in the Oval Office, if he found the time to eat at all. Then he would continue working through the afternoon, and often straight through dinner. He was a quick and attentive reader, able to go through piles of briefs at an astonishing rate. He was also a naturally curious individual, interested in absorbing all sides of an issue before rendering a decision. At night he relaxed by playing cards or watching the news on television. He and Mamie liked having friends over, and they would sometimes go up to the solarium on the White House roof, where Eisenhower enjoyed cooking steaks on a grill.

Mamie kept just as busy as her husband, managing the White House staff and answering scores of letters. Just as she had done when he was an up-and-coming military commander, she went to great pains to provide Eisenhower with as much support as he required. She charmed leaders and other powerful figures from all over the world when they came to the White House, and she became one of the most popular First Ladies in history.

His vice president, Richard Nixon, handled matters in Washington while Eisenhower did what he could from his hospital room. He remained in the hospital for six weeks. Then he went to Washington briefly and finally to his home in Gettysburg for the last stage of his recuperation. Since he had always been in relatively good health, he recovered from the heart attack and was back in the White House by late December, as busy as ever. In 1956 he had to return to the hospital again, this time for surgery caused by an inflammation in his small intestine. But it was a relatively minor operation, and he recovered quickly and went on with his duties.

Nevertheless, many were wondering if Eisenhower, due to health concerns, would be running for a second term as president. Even Eisenhower was not sure, but when he surveyed the field of other candidates later that year, he decided he had no choice. He still felt he was the best man for the job. With his popularity among the American people as high as ever, this was good news for the Republican Party. The Democrats, however, had no intention of giving up without a fight.

*T*he Democrats decided that the best way to successfully oppose Eisenhower was to create a rematch of the 1952 election, and they once again gave the nomination to Adlai Stevenson. He was no longer the governor of Illinois. After his defeat in 1952 he became a kind of journalist at large, traveling to many countries and writing articles about his experiences. Part of his campaign strategy in 1956 was to use these travels to show that he was now more aware of current events around the globe, having met with many foreign leaders during his journeys.

The Democratic Party once again nominated Adlai Stevenson to be Eisenhower's opponent in the presidential election of 1956.

The problem for Stevenson was that, just as in 1952, he was going against an enormously popular figure. Few people bought into the idea that Eisenhower's health was a serious risk to his ability to serve as president. Furthermore, Eisenhower's vice president, Richard Nixon, had proven himself more than capable of handling the affairs of state while Eisenhower was recovering from his heart attack. So, in the terrible event that Eisenhower should become ill again, the presidency would be transferred to someone with experience.

On election day—November 7, 1956—Eisenhower overwhelmed the hapless Stevenson, winning all but seven states and earning 57.4 percent of the popular vote. He even won the state of Louisiana, becoming the first Republican to do so since 1876. It was one of the most lopsided election victories in the history of the presidency.

Eisenhower's second victory over Stevenson was one of the most lopsided landslides in presidential history. Here, Eisenhower greets thousands of well-wishers on Inauguration Day, January 21, 1957.

Crisis in Lebanon

In early 1957, after Eisenhower had won the election but before he had technically begun his second term, he directed the creation of the Eisenhower Doctrine. It was a policy by which foreign

Eisenhower kept a rigid schedule as president, rising early every morning and rarely getting to his desk in the Oval Office later than eight o'clock.

nations could request assistance—military, financial, or otherwise—in the event that they were being threatened or attacked by communist forces. The one and only time during Eisenhower's presidency that the doctrine came into effect was in mid–1958, when the Middle Eastern nation of Lebanon became divided within itself and, as a result, the target of outside governments.

It started with a power struggle between Lebanon's president, Camille Chamoun, and the country's prime minister, Rashid Karami. It led to a mild civil war within Lebanese communities. Then, in July, the government of Iraq, a neighboring nation that was previously sympathetic to Chamoun, was toppled, and Chamoun began to sense a very dangerous situation developing. With the Eisenhower Doctrine in mind, Chamoun asked Eisenhower for help. Eisenhower sent over roughly 14,000 troops, and the situation was under control by the following October. There was only a handful of American casualties, and Eisenhower considered the mission an overwhelming success. He also wanted to make it clear that America could be counted on, whereas communist governments could not. One Eisenhower biographer noted that "Eisenhower wanted to impress [Egyptian president] Gamal Nasser, and to show him that he could not count on the Soviets, in order to give him 'food for thought.'"

A Revolution in Cuba

By the 1950s many of the nations in Latin America were being ruled not by democratic governments but by brutal dictatorships, usually with the aid of a military that was more interested in serving the demands of the dictator than the needs of the people. One such example was Cuba, which was under the control of

Fulgencio Batista. Batista ran the nation with shameless corruption. He was more interested in providing a vacation spot for foreign travelers than in tending to the needs of the Cuban people.

One Cuban citizen who dreamed of seeing Batista removed from office was Fidel Castro. Portraying himself as a hero of the people, he formed a ragtag band of revolutionaries and tried several times to overthrow the Batista regime. Although he failed in his first few attempts, he knew most of the Cuban people were behind him. Finally, on January 1, 1959, he and his forces entered the Cuban capital of Havana while Batista fled the country. At the young age of thirty-two, Castro became Cuba's new leader.

Eisenhower kept careful watch on Castro and his followers. He knew little about the man and wasn't sure what to make of him. Castro promised real change, vowing to form a government that would work hard to make life better for the average Cuban. In time, however, it was clear that he was as ruthless as Batista. He held publicly televised trials of his enemies, often executing them while his countrymen watched. He also removed any sections of the Cuban government that posed

Eisenhower was happy to see the repressive regime of Fulgencio Batista toppled in Cuba in 1959. However, he wasn't sure if the man responsible for it, Fidel Castro (above), would be much better.

THE CUBAN MISSILE CRISIS

The cold war never came closer to heating up than it did in October 1962, in an eerie near-fulfillment of Eisenhower's conviction that both Fidel Castro and Nikita Khrushchev posed a grave threat to the safety of the free world. Not long after Castro took power in Cuba and tried unsuccessfully to forge a relationship with the United States, he allied himself with the communist leadership in the Soviet Union. Khrushchev quickly realized that having an alliance with Castro was certainly valuable in one respect—Cuba was geographically very close to the United States, less than 100 miles from the coast of Florida. He ultimately made a deal with Castro to begin setting up Soviet missiles in Cuba—missiles that could easily reach any number of major U.S. cities. American intelligence services quickly learned of this, and then-president John F. Kennedy insisted that the missiles be removed. A period of heightened tension followed. Khrushchev eventually ordered that the missiles be removed.

a threat to him. It became obvious that he believed in government control over personal freedoms, and Eisenhower knew what that meant—communism.

Eisenhower decided that Castro was very dangerous and no friend of the United States, so he ordered that the **CIA** begin making plans to eliminate him. When Castro began developing a relationship with the Soviet Union, tensions between him and the American government increased. Eisenhower considered having him overthrown. As he noted in his presidential diaries, he had a meeting with the director of his National Security Council in order to "approve [a] directive requiring all departments to study applicability of our policies in light of global unrest as evidenced in . . . actions of Castro in Cuba." Eisenhower would not achieve his goal of removing Castro from power during his time in the White House, but subsequent presidents would try—unsuccessfully—to do the same. In the end Castro would rule Cuba for half a century.

A Second Chance for World Peace . . . Almost

Always deeply disappointed by how poorly the Open Skies talks had gone, Eisenhower asked Soviet leaders several times if they would be interested in meeting again. He still hoped to create some kind of agreement with them that would set the groundwork for a peaceful future. In early 1959 the Soviets indicated that they were open to another summit. Eisenhower was delighted, and the meeting was planned for May 16 in Paris. It became known as the Paris Summit.

In the months beforehand the United States had been regularly sending planes over the Soviet Union for the purpose of gathering information (mostly in the form of aerial photographs) on the state of the Soviet military. Eisenhower simply wanted to know what their capabilities were; he was not looking for targets to attack. Interestingly, the Soviets knew about many of these flights; this kind of arrangement was very much what Eisenhower had proposed in the Open Skies agreement in the first place. The Soviets were informed of these flying missions as a show of good faith, to let them know that the flights weren't being done behind their backs.

Then, just weeks before the May 16 summit in Paris, something went horribly wrong. Eisenhower gave the okay for a spy flight that the Soviets weren't told about, and the Soviets shot the plane down. When Khrushchev accused America of spying, Eisenhower denied knowing anything about it. A short time later, however, he was forced to admit that he did. This seriously hurt Eisenhower's credibility, and with the summit only weeks away, it could not have come at a worse time. Still, he didn't believe that Khrushchev was angry. As historian Geoffrey Perret wrote in his book *Eisenhower*, "On May 14, Eisenhower departed for Paris, having convinced himself that Khrushchev's furious denunciation of American espionage, provocation and general bad faith were a theatrical performance."

He was wrong. When the Soviets arrived, an enraged Khrushchev demanded not only that everyone involved in the flight be relieved of duty but also that Eisenhower issue a public apology. Eisenhower had no intention of doing any of these things. Knowing that the Soviets were conducting several secretive missions of their own for the same reasons, he found Khrushchev's outburst ridiculous. In an attempt to be reasonable, he pointed out to Khrushchev that secret flyovers would not have been necessary if he'd just agreed to the Open Skies plan in the first place. Khrushchev wasn't interested in such arguments, and he stormed out of the summit before it even got started. Depressed, Eisenhower went back to the United States having made no progress, and he would never again get a chance to meet with Soviet leaders. He never had the opportunity to negotiate a test-ban treaty—an agreement with the Soviets to ban the testing of atomic devices except underground—which was one of his greatest hopes as president.

THE LITTLE ROCK NINE

In late 1957 Eisenhower found himself involved in a sticky civil rights issue on the domestic front. Three years earlier the U.S. Supreme Court had handed down a landmark decision that eradicated the separate but equal ruling, which stated that it was constitutional for people to be segregated into different facilities based on their race as long as those facilities were of equal quality. The federal government knew it would take some time for this decision to be implemented. But the judges who handed down the decision expected it to be carried out in a reasonable and timely manner.

The Little Rock Nine had to be escorted to and from school to avoid being physically harmed. When riots erupted around the town in protest, Eisenhower ordered the Arkansas National Guard to quell the violence.

In the city of Little Rock, Arkansas, the first year of formal **integration** was scheduled to occur at the beginning of the 1957 school year. However, when black students showed up at Central High on September 3—the first day—they found the entryways blocked by the Arkansas National Guard, by order of the governor, Orval Faubus. As a professional politician Faubus was eager to make sure he got reelected when he had to run for another term. And in the South many voters did not look favorably on politicians who were friendly to blacks or other minorities.

A few weeks later, on September 20, Faubus was ordered to remove the National Guard blockade and honor the new Court ruling. The following Monday, the twenty-third, nine black students—eventually known as the Little Rock Nine—slipped quietly into a little-used entrance in order to attend classes. When word of this got out, the city of Little Rock exploded with riots and other hostilities. In response, Eisenhower ordered the Arkansas National Guard to stop the violence. To make sure his orders were obeyed, he sent down a thousand federal troops as well. Soldiers remained in Little Rock for the entire school year, some escorting the nine students to and from classes each day.

THE SPACE RACE

In early 1957 the Soviet Union shocked the world when it successfully sent the first human-made satellite, named Sputnik 1, into outer space. Confident that they were ahead of the Soviets in every way, Americans were aghast. To make matters worse, as Sputnik traveled into the frigid darkness, it began sending signals back to its base—signals that could be heard by many Americans over their radios. Since this was at the height of the cold war, word spread throughout the country and caused

WELCOME TO THE CLUB—
AMERICA GAINS TWO NEW STATES

At the beginning of Eisenhower's administration, America had only forty-eight states. At the end the nation had two more—Alaska and Hawaii. The Alaskan territory was purchased by the American government in 1867 and governed largely by the military, after having been ruled throughout the 1800s both by Russia and the United States at various times. The population increased during World War II, when U.S. forces built several military bases in the region. The government formally approved Alaska as the forty-ninth state in 1958, but it was not made official until January 1959. Both President Grover Cleveland and President William McKinley considered making Hawaii a U.S. territory in the late 1800s, but it didn't become one until 1900. In 1959 the federal government asked Hawaiian residents to vote on the possibility of American statehood, and the vast majority (94 percent) approved it. Eisenhower signed the Hawaii Admission Act into law on March 18, making it the fiftieth state.

widespread panic. Many wondered, if the Soviets could transmit signals through their radios, what else could they do? Perhaps they had the capability to send guided missiles into major U.S. cities. Maybe this was the start of a military invasion. These fears were multiplied the next month when the Soviet Union sent a larger and more powerful satellite into orbit.

In the face of public demand that something be done, Eisenhower remained levelheaded. One of his biographers, Michael Korda, wrote that "although Ike calmly declared that Sputnik did not 'raise his apprehensions,' he appeared to be the only person in the United States who felt that way." Based on intelligence that he was receiving, he did not believe there was any genuine military threat to be addressed. Furthermore, he was not eager to pour government money into an American space program just for the sake of competing with the Soviets, or for its own sake. American scientists were already working on their own spacecrafts, and Eisenhower was comfortable with their progress. But the average American did not share his relaxed composure, and the outcry continued. Finally, Eisenhower authorized an increase in the spending for American space effort.

As a result of being rushed, the United States launched a satellite in December, called the Vanguard, well before it was ready, and it quickly fell back to Earth in a fiery crash. Because of this huge embarrassment for the United States, those who headed the space program were determined not to be hastened in their next attempt. In January 1958 they launched their new satellite, Explorer 1, which reached orbit without any difficulties.

LATER YEARS

Even if Eisenhower had wanted to run for a third term as president, he would have been unable to. According to the Twenty-second Amendment to the U.S. Constitution, which was added in 1951, a president was allowed to serve only two terms. In Eisenhower's case, this likely would not have mattered much. There is little doubt that he was tired of the job by the end of his second term. He had done his duty to his country both as a soldier and a politician. Now it was time to begin the final stage of his life.

HELPING NIXON . . . OR NOT

With the 1960 election fast approaching, the Republicans had to nominate someone to make a presidential run. They had no illusions about finding a candidate as popular as Eisenhower had been; he was still a favorite of the American voters, even after his second term. In the end they decided to nominate Richard Nixon, who had been Eisenhower's vice president. The Republicans hoped that some of Eisenhower's popularity would somehow rub off on Nixon, given that he had been the vice president for so long. Also, Nixon was a very experienced politician at that point, knowledgeable of the way things worked in Washington. In addition, he was very intelligent and could be very charming—a trait that he often concealed from the public and, in fact, from many who worked for and with him.

It is customary for an outgoing president to campaign, to some degree, for the new nominee of his own party. Since Nixon was Eisenhower's vice president, the Republican Party assumed that Eisenhower would make some public appearances on Nixon's behalf. But there was a problem—Eisenhower and Nixon were not very close. They never really became friends in spite of the eight years they served together. Some even thought that Eisenhower disliked Nixon. Nixon had been a faithful and dutiful vice president, supporting Eisenhower's plans and decisions without question. If he ever disagreed with Eisenhower, he certainly did not do so publicly.

Nevertheless, Eisenhower did not put forth his best effort to get Nixon elected. If he was forced to make a choice between Nixon and his Democratic opponent, Senator John F. Kennedy, he would undoubtedly support Nixon, out of loyalty to

By all accounts, Eisenhower's vice president, Richard Nixon (left), executed the duties of his job faithfully and earnestly, supporting the president on all important matters. Nevertheless, he and Eisenhower never shared a close relationship.

the Republican Party rather than to Nixon himself. The truth was that Eisenhower didn't like either candidate. He also had issues with his age and his health. His wife, Mamie, had quietly asked the Nixon campaign staff not to make many appearance requests of her husband. As a result, this, too, led many to believe that Eisenhower did not back Nixon's presidential hopes.

Ironically, when Eisenhower did speak out during the campaign, he sometimes said things that hurt Nixon rather than helped him. One famous example was when he was asked by a reporter what major decisions he had made in which Nixon had played a role. Eisenhower replied, "If you give me a week, I might think of one." This comment was particularly damaging to Nixon because the Republicans were trying to convince the American people that he was experienced in presidential affairs—a very

AN EISENHOWER–NIXON MARRIAGE?

In spite of the fact that Dwight Eisenhower and Richard Nixon never formed a particularly close relationship, one member from each of their families managed to do a little better—Dwight David Eisenhower II, Eisenhower's grandson, met Julie Nixon, Richard Nixon's daughter, during the 1956 Republican National Convention in San Francisco. They married in December 1968 and went on to have three children. By this time Julie's father had been elected president, and she became known for speaking out publicly on political subjects. She also became an author and editor of the renowned magazine *The Saturday Evening Post*. Eisenhower's son was also an author as well as an officer in the Naval Reserves.

important factor against the less-experienced Kennedy. Another blunder on Eisenhower's part was when Nixon went on television to debate Kennedy over current issues, and Eisenhower said that he didn't even bother to watch the debate. The very few times that Eisenhower did campaign for Nixon, he spent most of the time talking about his own accomplishments as president rather than those of Nixon. In the end Nixon lost the election to Kennedy by a narrow margin, and Kennedy was sworn in as the nation's thirty-fifth president in January 1961.

Massachusetts Democrat John F. Kennedy would succeed Eisenhower as president following the election of 1960, beating out Nixon in one of the narrowest margins in history.

Back Home

On January 20 Eisenhower gave a final briefing to incoming President Kennedy. They spoke about the most pressing matters of state, both foreign and domestic, and Eisenhower gave him some general advice on how best to serve the country. Then Eisenhower and Mamie left the White House for the last time, taking a relatively short—less than 100 miles—car ride to their home in Gettysburg. His presidency was finally over.

In the years that followed, Eisenhower would be asked to come back to the White House from time to time. Since he had had eight years of experience as president and many more as a general, his advice was highly sought after. Kennedy and the president who followed him, Lyndon Johnson, often consulted with him on military matters. Both men dealt with many of the same issues that Eisenhower had, including—perhaps most notably—the war in Vietnam. Johnson greatly expanded America's involvement in that war. According to Eisenhower, the best way for a president to take part in a war was to put smart and experienced generals in the field, then give them the troops and weaponry they needed to win. Eisenhower was frequently irritated by Johnson's relatively poor handling of Vietnam.

Eisenhower was invited back to the White House many times after his presidency ended, often to consult on military matters. Here he is seen speaking with President Lyndon B. Johnson in 1965.

Back in Gettysburg Eisenhower settled into a comfortable life at home. He still loved to cook and spend time in his garden, and he had taken up painting. He admitted on many occasions that he wasn't very good at it, but he found the act of painting particularly relaxing. He also enjoyed visits from friends and family. He had several grandchildren by this time, and he would sit and read to them. He and Mamie often played board games together on the sun porch, battling each other at Scrabble or chess. He had a large piece of property, and he bought some cattle to manage—evidence that the Abilene farm boy inside him was still alive and well. He also enjoyed hunting in and around the wooded sections of his land. And, of course, he still golfed when the urge struck. Eisenhower would forever be associated with the game by historians and the public alike.

The health problems that he had developed while president worsened in his final years. In November 1965 he had yet another heart attack. He recovered from this one and went on with his retirement, but he was clearly slowing down. In April 1968 he had another, and after this attack, his heart gradually failed. He did his best to take it easy, but the end was drawing near. Eventually he was admitted to the Walter Reed Army Medical Center in Washington, D.C., where he died on March 28, 1969. His last words were believed to be "I want to go—God take me." His remains lay in state inside the rotunda of the Capitol for a brief period, then were taken by train back to Abilene, where he was buried on the grounds of his presidential library.

Few Americans had a greater impact on the country than Dwight Eisenhower. As a young military officer, he deeply impressed the men at the highest levels of the U.S. Army. As a general, he built an army of unprecedented strength—one that

Mamie's Later Years

Mamie Eisenhower continued to live in the Gettysburg house for many years after Eisenhower's death. She lived quietly, spending time with friends and family and, for the most part, staying out of the limelight. In the late 1970s she moved back to Washington, D.C., to a modest apartment. After suffering a stroke in 1979, she was taken to Walter Reed Army Medical Center—the same place where Eisenhower had been treated for heart disease—and died just over a month later. She was then buried next to Eisenhower in Abilene. To her final days she remained one of America's most beloved First Ladies.

would change America's military from a relatively small force to the greatest superpower in human history. He designed the very plans that led to victory in the bloodiest and costliest conflict of the twentieth century. Then, as president, he kept America strong on the global stage while overseeing a staggering period of prosperity and growth. And all along he did this with common sense, decency, and humility. To Eisenhower, he was merely doing his duty.

Dwight D. Eisenhower's impact on the United States during the twentieth century is almost impossible to estimate. As both a general and a president, he led the nation through some of its darkest hours.

1890
Born in Denison, Texas,
on October 14

1915
Graduates from West Point
Military Academy

1916
Marries Mamie Geneva
Doud on July 1

1926
Graduates from the General
Command and Staff School

1890

1952

Wins the presidential election in November against Democratic opponent Adlai Stevenson

1956

Wins a second presidential election in November, again beating Democratic opponent Adlai Stevenson

1969

Dies after prolonged health problems at Walter Reed Army Medical Center on March 28

1970

NOTES

CHAPTER ONE

p.8, "My father legislated the matter with the traditional hickory switch . . .": Dwight D. Eisenhower, *At Ease: Stories I Tell to Friends*. Garden City, NY: Doubleday and Company, 1967, p. 51.

p.9, "If someone's been guilty of despicable actions . . .": Dwight D. Eisenhower, *At Ease: Stories I Tell to Friends*, p. 52.

p.16, "The man who ranked above me in the West Point examinations . . .": Dwight D. Eisenhower, *At Ease: Stories I Tell to Friends*, p. 106.

p.19, "He was a very complex man . . .": John S. D. Eisenhower, *General Ike: A Personal Reminiscence*. New York: Free Press, 2003, p. 179.

CHAPTER TWO

p.29, "Adding to Patton's larger-than-life image in the Army . . .": John S. D. Eisenhower, p. 3.

p.31, "It was not an inviting place, especially for Mamie . . .": John S. D. Eisenhower, p. 7.

p.33, ". . . once had written": Harry C. Butcher, *My Three Years with Eisenhower: The Personal Diary of Captain Harry C. Butcher, USNR, Naval Aide to General Eisenhower*. New York: Simon and Schuster, 1946, p. 874.

p.37, "Most of those who joined the Nazis did so because . . .": Erhardt Knorpel as quoted in William Sheridan Allen, *The Nazi Seizure of Power: The Experience of a Single German Town, 1930–1935*. New York: New Viewpoints, 1973, p. 78.

p.38, "This was due to the vision and determination of one man . . .": Dwight D. Eisenhower, *Crusade in Europe*. Garden City, NY: Doubleday and Company, 1948, p. 16.

CHAPTER THREE

p.42, "I was certain that the United States would be drawn . . .": Dwight D. Eisenhower, *Crusade in Europe*, p. 5.

p.44, "The African venture was looked upon as diversionary . . .": Dwight D. Eisenhower, *Crusade in Europe*, p. 72.

p.47, "Before breakfast Ike received a message relayed from Algiers . . .": Harry C. Butcher, p. 371.

p.48, "Ike wandered through them, stepping over packs, guns . . .": Harry C. Butcher, p. 566.

p.52, ". . . crowded with cheering men and women . . .": Harry C. Butcher, p. 870.

Chapter Four

p.62, "We must show the wickedness of purpose in the communist promises . . .":
Dwight D. Eisenhower, as quoted in Robert H. Ferrell (editor), *The Eisenhower
Diaries*. New York: W. W. Norton and Company, 1981, p. 223.

p.63, "The power of the bomb is not of itself . . .": Dwight D. Eisenhower, as quoted in
Robert H. Ferrell (editor), p. 277.

p.68, "Krushchev said the idea was nothing more than a bald espionage plot . . .":
Stephen E. Ambrose, *Eisenhower, Soldier and President: The Renowned
One-Volume Life*. New York: Touchstone Books, 1990, p. 393.

p.70, "By the summer of 1946, the White House was under considerable pressure . . .":
Ellen Schrecker, *The Age of McCarthyism: A Brief History with Documents*.
New York: Bedford Books, 1994, p. 7.

Chapter Five

p.79, "Eisenhower wanted to impress [Egyptian president] Gamal Nasser . . .":
Stephen E. Ambrose, *Eisenhower, Soldier and President: The Renowned
One-Volume Life*. New York: Touchstone Books, 1990, p. 469.

p.82, ". . . directive requiring all departments to study applicability . . .": Dwight D.
Eisenhower, as quoted in Robert H. Ferrell (editor), p. 378.

p.83, ". . . Eisenhower departed for Paris, having convinced himself . . .": Geoffrey
Perret, *Eisenhower*. New York: Random House, 1999, p. 583.

p.87, ". . . although Ike calmly declared that Sputnik did not . . .": Michael Korda,
Ike: An American Hero. New York: HarperCollins, 2007, pp. 699–700.

Chapter Six

p.90, "If you give me a week, I might think . . .": Michael Korda, p. 716.

p.93, "I want to go —God take me.": Dwight D. Eisenhower as quoted in Geoffrey
Perret, p. 608

GLOSSARY

Allied Powers group of nations that formed the eventual victorious side in World Wars I and II.

armistice an agreement to halt hostilities during a war, similar to a truce

capitalism an economic system in which most businesses are owned by private citizens rather than the government

censure to formally condemn

Central Intelligence Agency agency responsible for providing national security intelligence

Central Powers group of nations that formed the eventual losing side in World War I

cold war term used to describe the adversarial relationship between the United States and Russia following World War II that lasted more than four decades

containment U.S. foreign policy that aimed to prevent the spread of communism.

communism a social and economic system in which people put their individual rights and freedoms second to the "greater good" of their community

Congress the legislative branch of the U.S. government, made up of two parts—the Senate and the House of Representatives

creamery part of the farming industry, a creamery is where dairy products such as cream, butter, and cheese are processed

Democratic Party One of the two major political parties in the United States, considered the more liberal and progressive, and in favor of a larger government

Great Depression period of economic stagnation in America that began with the stock market crash of October 1929 and lasted until roughly 1939, the onset of World War II

Holocaust the murder of millions of Jews and others in secret death camps by the Nazis during World War II

House of Representatives one of the two parts of the U.S. Congress; considered the lower of the two

inflation a general, continuous increase in prices

integration act of combining racial groups into a community

Jehovah's Witnesses a religion begun in the United States during the late nineteenth century that is strongly pacifist and only casually recognizes the authority of governments

McCarthyism the act of accusing someone, or a group of people, of disloyalty without having any solid proof, inspired by the acts of Wisconsin senator Joseph McCarthy to expose all those in American government (and several other American organizations) whom he believed to have affiliations with the Communist Party

Mennonites a religious sect that originated in Europe in the sixteenth century from the Protestant faith; Mennonites refused to serve in the military

NATO acronym for the North Atlantic Treaty Organization, made up of twelve nations who signed an agreement in April 1949 to support one another against attacks from other countries

Nazi Party German political party led by Adolf Hitler before and during World War II

Republican Party one of the two major political parties in the United States, considered the more conservative and in favor of a smaller government

River Brethren a sect of the Mennonite religion that was formed by German colonists in Pennsylvania in the late eighteenth century

U.S. Senate one of the two parts of the U.S. Congress; considered the upper of the two

State Department agency of the U.S. government that deals with matters concerning foreign countries.

Treaty of Versailles agreement that Germany was forced to sign following World War I, stating that Germany was responsible for the war and requiring it to pay reparations for the damage caused

Vietnam War a conflict primarily between the northern and southern halves of Vietnam that also involved aid from the United States plus several other allied nations

Further Information

Books

Adams, Simon. *World War II*. New York: DK Children's Books, 2007.

Aronson, Billy. *Richard Nixon*. New York: Marshall Cavendish, 2008.

Birkner, Michael J. *Dwight D. Eisenhower, America's 34th President*. Danbury, CT: Children's Press, 2005.

Grant, R. G. *The Cold War*. London, England: Arcturus Publishing, 2007.

Wagner, Melissa, and Dan Bryant. *The Big Book of World War II: Fascinating Facts about WWII Including Maps, Historic Photographs, and Timelines*. Philadelphia, PA: Running Press Kids, 2009.

DVDs

The Big Picture: The Dwight D. Eisenhower Story. Washington, D.C.: National Archives and Records Administration, 2008.

Biography: Dwight D. Eisenhower. New York: A&E Home Video, 2005.

Ike: Countdown to D-Day. Culver City, CA: Sony Pictures, 2004.

WEBSITES

Dwight D. Eisenhower Presidential Library and Museum

www.eisenhower.archives.gov/

Official site of the Dwight D. Eisenhower Presidential and Library Museum. A tremendous website with excellent content, beautifully presented. Suitable for all ages.

World War II

www.socialstudiesforkids.com/subjects/worldwarii.htm

Excellent, content-rich site for children on all aspects of World War II. Includes information on the Pearl Harbor attack, the Holocaust, famous figures, the atomic bombs dropped on Hiroshima and Nagasaki, and much more.

Cold War

www.neok12.com/Cold-War.htm

NeoK12 page about the cold war. Very child-friendly, with lots of short videos covering all aspects of this tense period in world history.

BIBLIOGRAPHY

Allen, William Sheridan. *The Nazi Seizure of Power: The Experience of a Single German Town, 1930–1935*. New York: New Viewpoints, 1973.

Ambrose, Stephen E. *D-Day: June 6, 1944: The Climactic Battle of World War II*. New York: Touchstone Books, 1994.

Ambrose, Stephen E. *Eisenhower, Soldier and President: The Renowned One-Volume Life*. New York: Touchstone Books, 1990.

Black, Conrad. *Richard M. Nixon: A Life in Full*. New York: PublicAffairs, 2007.

Butcher, Harry C. *My Three Years with Fisenhower: The Personal Diary of Captain Harry C. Butcher, USNR, Naval Aide to General Eisenhower*. New York: Simon and Schuster, 1946.

Dollinger, Hans. *The Decline and Fall of Nazi Germany and Imperial Japan: A Pictorial History of the Final Days of World War II*. New York: Bonanza Books, 1965.

Eisenhower, Dwight D. *At Ease: Stories I Tell to Friends*. Garden City, NY: Doubleday and Company, 1967.

Eisenhower, Dwight D. *Crusade in Europe*. Garden City, NY: Doubleday and Company, 1948.

Eisenhower, John S. D. *General Ike: A Personal Reminiscence*. New York: Free Press, 2003.

Ferguson, Niall. *The Pity of War: Explaining World War I*. New York: Basic Books, 1999.

Ferrell, Robert H. (editor). *The Eisenhower Diaries*. New York: W. W. Norton and Company, 1981.

Gilbert, Martin. *The Second World War: A Complete History*. New York: Henry Holt and Company, 2004.

Korda, Michael. *Ike: An American Hero*. New York: HarperCollins, 2007.

McCullough, David. *Truman*. New York: Simon and Schuster, 1992.

Perret, Geoffrey. *Eisenhower*. New York: Random House, 1999.

Schrecker, Ellen. *The Age of McCarthyism: A Brief History with Documents*. New York: Bedford Books, 1994.

Weinberg, Gerhard L. *A World at Arms: A Global History of World War II*. Cambridge, UK: Cambridge University Press, 1994.

INDEX

Pages in **boldface** are illustrations.

★ ★ ★ ★ ★ ★ ★ ★ ★ ★ ★ ★ ★ ★ ★ ★ ★ ★ ★

ABOUT THE AUTHOR

Wil Mara is the award-winning author of more than a hundred books. He has written both fiction and nonfiction, for children and adults. More information about his work can be found at www.wilmara.com.